THE
SPIRITUAL HUNT

ARTHUR RIMBAUD

THE
SPIRITUAL
HUNT

TRANSLATED
BY
EMINE ERSOY

NEW YORK
MERCURIAL EDITIONS
MMXXIV

INTRODUCTION

Among the unpublished texts and correspondence that Paul Verlaine left behind at his in-laws' on Rue Nicolet when he abandoned his wife and son on July 7th, 1872, was a manuscript by Arthur Rimbaud titled La Chasse Spirituelle (The Spiritual Hunt). *Some months later, in November, Verlaine wrote two letters from London asking for the retrieval of the pages he left in Paris: the first to his friend Edmon Lepelletier and the second to Philippe Burty.*

After writing to Lepelletier, Verlaine learned that his wife, Mathilde, had entrusted Burty with the so-called "martyric" letters from Rimbaud, hoping that Verlaine's mother would not come across this potentially damning correspondence. These letters may very well have been intermixed with the loose manuscript leaflets comprising the poet's latest work, The Spiritual Hunt. *It seemed to be Verlaine's intention to create confusion between the two when he explained to Burty, against all plausibility, that the letters Mathilde had found weren't letters at all, but rather flyaway pages of Rimbaud's manuscript.*

Without being privy to Burty's reply, one cannot say whether he had indeed been the custodian of all or part of the documents Verlaine left so carelessly in Paris. In any case, he never returned the papers to Verlaine as requested. The handing over of these documents to Burty, if it took place at all, could only have been conditional. How else could Mathilde Mauté, determined as she was to pursue legal judgment against her absent husband, relinquish the correspondence which substantiated the narrative she'd put forth since October 2ⁿᵈ to justify her demand for a divorce?

One could easily suppose, however, that even if Mathilde Mauté's solicitor wanted to use Rimbaud's letters to assist his client, he may not have seen any point in fattening his briefcase with the manuscript of The Spiritual Hunt, *which did not implicate Verlaine in any way.*

What, then, became of this manuscript? Up until this moment, scholars have seemed to agree that it was lost forever. Indeed, for seventy-seven years, its presence had not been indicated in any private or public collection, in any sale, in the catalog of no library nor bookseller; even the most dogged collectors seemed inclined to admit to its extinction.

They were wrong. There exists another manuscript of The Spiritual Hunt *- perhaps there exist even two. For motives it does not behoove us to interrogate, the bearers of these documents of exceptional value and interest do not wish to identify themselves. May the present publication, made possible by a series of coincidences, incite them to make themselves known, henceforth less possessive over the secret of their Rimbaldian riches.*

From what we can tell, the composition of The Spiritual Hunt *took place over the course of the early months of 1872. Perhaps a close examination of the manuscript and a comparison of other texts by Rimbaud would allow for a more precise estimation, but as it stands our only recourse is an inspection of its style, an attentive listening.*

Rimbaud's letter to Ernest Delahaye dated "Parmerde, Juinphe 72" makes us think it was in May 1872, at Rue Monsieur-le-Prince, that The Spiritual Hunt *was written. Among Rimbaud's epistolary instructions to Delahaye is the line:*

Do not confine yourself to offices and family homes

And further aphorisms as Rimbaud arranged them:

The brutalities must be enacted far away from here. Far be it from me to peddle any cure, but I do think regularity offers no consolation from the pitiful days.

*Such lines signal the same ethic expressed from the very begin-
ning of* The Spiritual Hunt. *But that is not the only analogy
that surfaces between the manuscript and the Juinphe letter.*

*Notwithstanding the fact that any poetic fragment of Rimbaud's
implies more deliberation and overall more attentiveness by the
author than does his correspondence, one can recognize an air in
the below narrative to Delahaye quite similar to the one conjured
by certain parts of* The Spiritual Hunt:

Last month, my room on rue Monsieur-le-Prince looked over
the schoolyard of the Lycée Saint-Louis. There were huge
sheds under my narrow window. At three in the morning
the candle pales: the birds all scream at once in the trees: it's
over. No more work. I had to look at the trees, the sky, taken
over by this unutterable hour, first of the morning. I looked at
the school dormitories, which were totally deaf. And already
the loud, halting, delicious noise of trucks on the boulevards -
I was smoking my pipe, all the while spitting on the roof tiles,
as my room was in the attic. At five, I went down to buy some
bread. Workers up and running everywhere. For me, it's time
to get drunk at the wineseller's...

It remains to be seen where The Spiritual Hunt *can be placed,
not in Rimbaud's oeuvre - such a word hardly applies - but rath-
er in the Rimbaldian storm. In this respect, there is no doubt:* The
Spiritual Hunt *governs and prefigures everything that the "mad
virgin" is immune to in* A Season In Hell. *It is no mere coinci-*

dence that the epithet "pagan", which Rimbaud had in mind for the book that was meant to become A Season in Hell, *figures in the title of a passage in* The Spiritual Hunt.

The references we could establish from one text to the other are many. Themes and images give each other cues:

I do not believe in family, duty, in the happinesses promised by esteem. *(The Spiritual Hunt)*

As to established happiness, domestic or not... no, I cannot. *(A Season in Hell)*

Our fleets will yet sail to the distant isles, new fields of honor for tomorrow. Catarrhous emperors will spit on slumbering crowds. Pirates and cutthroats will be immortalized. Who will we dream of? The barracks will spill waves of infected heroes in hygienic prairies, bored to death. The women await the invalids with gratitude. *(The Spiritual Hunt)*

My day is done; I'm leaving Europe. The sea air will burn my lungs; the lost climates will tan me... I will return with iron limbs... I'll have gold. I'll be idle and brutal. Women take care of these ferocious cripples on their return from warm countries. *(A Season in Hell)*

Idiotic songs ran circles in my head. *(The Spiritual Hunt)*

I loved idiotic paintings...unfashionable literature...stupid refrains, naive rhythms. *(A Season in Hell)*

We could multiply these citations, see the symmetrically opposed declarations:

I am indeed from here. *(The Spiritual Hunt,* Infirmities*)*

I am no longer of the world. *(A Season In Hell,* Night of Hell*)*

Just as A Season In Hell *exposes the freshest joy in the "deaf leap of the ferocious beast",* The Spiritual Hunt *ensnares, menaces, and wounds the hunter. Its final sentence, ("Surely it's not from around here"), will no doubt inspire new exegeses. For our part, we will abstain from offering or accepting any. We have never stopped sinking our heels into the conviction that Rimbaud systematically discourages attempts at interpretation or mobilization. His most prideful assertion: "It is oracle, what I'm saying", taunts the reader, for the oracle is ambiguous, and Rimbaud further feeds this mystery with a slew of denials and rejections. No one else has taken such advantage of the liberties Baudelaire wished to have seen inscribed in the Declaration of Human Rights: the right to contradict oneself and the right to go away.*

Pascal Pia, 1949

THE
SPIRITUAL HUNT

VAUDEVILLE

There was a time I would cry over vain attachments. I don't believe in family, duty, or the happinesses promised by esteem. Rancid soup, bland sweets, and angelic perfume of wardrobe avens. Let us discard temperaments, mismatched playthings - sanctioned sentimentalism - and not forget these precocious maledictions. No complacent attitudes, nor offices, nor prudent glory. No more heroism or honor restored. Hide away your wisdom and science, your treasures - your detestable pleas.

Too much I've remasticated your disdain, your pretexts, your aimless patience. I too have enjoyed easy delights - not long ago I could have been among the greats, full of rigor and principles. I can no longer laugh at these extravagant obsoletions.

I am furthering myself from the memory of these childish communions, these ingenious enchantments. Holidays. The countryside rectory smelled like washing-up and I paid my respects to the man hiding the conspiracies of his indifference under a marvelous fresco. Dear sickness! I walk up the boulevards engorged with vacant people. Vain and damp pleasures. The suburban creameries swoon over the scent of our metropolitan angels.

Our fleets will yet sail to distant isles, new fields of honor for tomorrow. Catarrhous emperors will spit on slumbering crowds. Pirates and cutthroats will be immortalized. Who will we dream of? The barracks will spill waves of infected heroes over hygienic prairies, bored to death. The women await the invalids with gratitude.

Magic of nauseating colors, trumpets which leather from blue abscesses the palms and mouths of noon killings, indecent and orderly. Generations of communiants will blemish their candor still. Hideously docile nature, rich and comfortable city, accessible arts, miserable fake pianos.

Madmen of the hours. Epileptics, you will live through the common dangers, arms thick with blood, legs open, lubricated, mouth to the ground: in evenings of too-human liberty.

Upon the exercise of routine gestures, transport of weapons and flags, towards the crumbling of the glory climax, at the ruinous dawn of authentic homelands you may be exhausted, like mothers.

PAGAN HOLIDAYS

On that day, disavowed, astray, dead to the hope of destined positions, advantages, glimpsed rots of the abyss - it must have been yesterday - I determined the aim of these decisions born from the mystification of debauch.

I'll forget the taste of anathema, the simple insult - for once - all the ferocities, the grotesque freneticisms, the cruel movements, and the vain blasphemes of childhood. With these eyes I see deserts chipped like scabs, battered by sky. A forest of silk and amber, still further away. I hear - why this betrayal of silence again in which I arrive royally - shameful melodies.

Must I keep suffering and drag myself there? I'll no longer be able to drink, but what exquisite rewards beyond the limits of this impoverished flesh. I will escape the ill-mannered day, the familial traps, the lamp of constrained and dishonest wakes, the conventional digestions, the peaceful noises behind a closed door, the extenuated city.

I wish to stammer the relinquishment of our definitive systems, of our cultures, riches of memory. To learn henceforth the oblivion of consented fictions, I mean the easy and mortal hours, of friendship, of practical recognitions.

I worship indifferent animals, splendid and errant like the ancient gods, under pitiless skies.

To abolish oneself, to lose oneself, to feel one's skin parch under the avid and envious gaze of puerile curiosities and - shamelessly - to devour oneself in the deepest dreams. Time: dementia of others! I will no longer scream towards you, full of logician wisdom. You will remain unaware of these forbidden revelations, the rhythms of this barbaric orchestra, my patience, my obstinance, my bitter royalty, my strength.

Floods devour the superior peoples and only a couple of well-meaning idiot maniacs can see on the bulwark of a scarlet wealth the fuming messengers of its obligations.

The old shorelines blur in the wind: the fraternal prairies noisy with the joy of insects.

I see without hesitation the quartz cliffs, guardians of riverless red and black valleys. I will murder the ordinary dream with cunning, science, bastard loves and humiliating tenderness. And they will be dancers once more, artists, ridiculous and beautiful. Sacrificing everything for a twilight murder at the end of a park in Babylon.

I will bend the iron bars of an occidental sky and follow the steps of mages and scorned prophets, in anguish over our devoured relatives. But of no relation to obsolete beliefs, to the destiny of absurd and ruined virtues - free.

The horror of indulgence precedes me. I will undo myself of elementary mannerisms. Cross my arms over the infinite. How simple it is! The superior barbarians had seen it all coming: liquidate wisdom and onward!

Soon, no more absence. Hearts will no longer be tortured. No more remedies. A force fed by silence, immobile. No more ancient will, no more backwards momentum. The implacable plain. The body still and vacant like a sanctuary. Turning one's gaze to the inner shadow. Sleeping on the magic carpet and head full of terrifying realities - lighter than the dream of a well-behaved child - mysterious illusions, I will erase myself deliciously.

Nave restored with gold, streamless, stormless, I will soon approach the venerated port from which the sun ventures out to our commercial continents, our docks, our fruitful tides, our stopovers, our dreary beaches.

I want to walk on tightropes towards this primordial wisdom and marvelous world.

But with a revolted heart, head full of muddy waters, a pitiful hunter: haunting the sickly shores where the sea breams brew. I must still want beyond the secular myths.

My regrets, my divergent presence, my cold reason, alas! And all the enthusiasms and the calculations, and the affectionate detours, the respectable economy, I will no longer be accountable for any of it. I will depart, banned for good, drunk, from the circle of actions glimmering with the arabesques of the deloused. I will remember the acrid scent of pious women. I will horse dream. I will adore the sacred goat, the clawed cats yowling of lust.

I will cling to the gas lamp of hopeless neighborhoods, I will walk up to the glare, feet in flames, I will trespass upon the consecutive rooms of a teeming empty temple and die destroying golden tubers and white birds.

Goodbye, catechism, worn-out loves!

I have cut off my right hand.

EDENS

Last prayer to the archangels rotting in my fevered woods. I stumble the sixty lives of the cycle. Finally I'll nail down my fixtures, my pursuits, my astrides - ordinary images forged in the discomfort of awakening. I confide in you my fictitious absences, a collection of savage words aflame. I have stammered famously through the picturesque curse of the senses.

Knee-deep in the stupid meadow I rattled the pistils, a sordid and complex child, enveloped with cold green vapors, stuck my raging arms in the vase of an atrocious tepidity brimmed with thick rosy worms. I learned the whistling of monsters, heroic verses, the mud-laughs from lakes of darkness, flowering castles of agony slept by soft, chaste princes. I counted the precious stones and airborne rivers lined with quicksand statues in tropical sea creeks, and haunted the fairground shacks where the ballerinas strangle themselves.

I felt the cravings of poor children. Head sonorous like a giant seashell, abandoned to the mornings after those orgies of fasting, spirit heavier than a cathedral. I questioned the wisdom of ancient marbles, tore apart the obscene shapes of grenades, and ruby streams trickled over my lips.

A smoking, acrid body. Desire, desperation, belated affliction, sticky kisses of exotic poison, leprosy, desperate embraces. Burning chalice, operatic airs, gladiators adorned for the popular hungers, sirens and sorceresses, hypocrite brides, priests swilling suspicious liqueurs at the sound of a gong, rustic seats for the salons. Viscous bubbles burst before my eyes, arrows of many colors nail me to a tailored ordeal. Older sisters with their exasperating solitude console the pathetic children and soft Jesuses tend to worn happiness.

Paradise as it should be, Cytherea, one hand to save me, and then, alone, calm in the sainfoin fields, I'll hear the back-then cries from behind the trees, the wind healer of expectations. I'll reach the sublime degree of brazen perfection. No longer hide from the world my errors and egotisms and unknown tenderness.

I settle the most infamous debts.

Venom cascades, whirlpool of red black snow, gust of foul breaths, carnival, cryptic tortoises, cancers and hydras made up in verdigris, mighty hounds, spayed roosters, lace; in the glorious sky shreds of flesh organize ascensions, hideous monkeys steal my clothes, arrows, gem rivers, shapeless flowers, bloody sap, blasted crystals, pastels dusty from obscure visions. Kangaroos jump in the town square and the freighters braid rosaries slipping over ember oceans.

Marine butterflies, Jamaicas, lemon trees, peppers from numb tropics, scented algae, pustules, honey sores, furious mammoths, serpents in heat devouring ship crews, velvet-speared cannibal flowers, delights, tortures.... Oh! Pity! Mercy, I will not start again.

None of this is really that serious.

INFIRMITIES

I will no longer tease the fevers and nightmares that made my body tremble and riled up my nerves. I know what I owe them.

I should have rejected needs, fears, doubts. I would have splendidly robbed nature and my species and my obscure parents. All I am is specimen - nothing more - bound to these domesticated viscera and to this doomed and degraded spirit. I am indeed from here.

Life is simple and yielding except for thought and this thirst. Could I carry on? The scholars and laborers surround me in a bitter and vertiginous orbit. The leaves push, the usual foods renew themselves and water and fire. I lost the ordinary traces. I shouldn't have.

From now on no beast can subdue me.

I return subdued to the welcome of an austere and comfortable home. I've embarrassed love's begging, altruistic hunger and the desire for brotherly presence. I caught sight of the voluptuous quietudes, eyes ringed with webs of mauve, orphan of equinoxes and inevitable tides, lunations and natural laws. Idiotic songs ran circles in my head. Schoolyard refrains, mechanical prayers useful for the hygiene of our adolescent bodies.

Fugitive from the limits of the absurd and manifest ignorances, in appeasement of the mysterious grasps, needs, duties, paltry generosities, and sterile combats shall forever be lost to me. Forsaken obstinate idiots, what will you make of this practical heritage, drunk from arguments, childish and secular like the rest of your kind?

Greasy smokes sputter the stench of journeys with no return, waste obstructs the gaping mouth of rivers; stomach ballooned, excrement, sour liquid, oozing remnants of monstrous cities.

The little girls staring stunned and dumb turn me red from shame.

Anathema to these penchants of diabolic fertility. Nature queen of hordes you have subdued us. Entire nights I ran after beatific visions - moon races, dull eclipses, perfect circles - pitiful outcome.

You who practice relative motions and remunerated efforts, you'll forget me. Gray cadavers, how to save you yet?

SWAMPS

Return to the sky friend of forever. Fatal disappointments rush to where they came from after an attempted rage against the forces. Banned from prudent capitals, deaf to truths. I can swallow their words and dusts, charlatans' delusions. But the monuments, testament to their spectacular misunderstanding, will crumble.

Time and her laughable accessories carry on. Nothing will be more than practical. The curves lose consciousness, the numbers, tamed in the old days, fall apart. Beyond the psychic guarantee of a brown and motherly earth, warm like a bird. Perhaps once more the uncertain brotherhood, vestige of primordial magics, permitted romance. Science, chemistry, frenesy, the pulverized stars will fall as gold dust over the ultimate revelations. What renewed heavens will the black barges drift under?

Figs are trampled on the ash beaches and the infected clouds ransack heaven's groves.

To take back tools and combat the path of duty.

Necktied Sundays on the boulevard of boredom.

In the orchestra of cruel yappings I was dismembered by the crowd. I looked for the fainting of the world; breathless, eyes swollen with itch, rhythm of the last forces accounted for. The perfect burst of fire escaped me and everything was intact: comedic royalties, the people's bewilderments. Cults, stones, trees, spurned hearts, will I feel your strange presence again - your pride, your disdain?

In hunting this sweet magic I forgot about weapons, ruses, and charms. I return blind, hands frozen and dead, to the ominous clearing of fallen trees, with no scintillating prey to boast, no trophies. I will stuff myself with revulsions - and what else is there to do, left to the magnificent brutalities, to

disciplines, to the demands of the era gaping at these hard-
ened feet.

I saw myself kneeled at the crossing of ancient disturbances,
shivering, scepter in hand, scarlet crowned, in the exacting
adornment of messiahs. Must one get up today, run, fuss?
That's the old fashion.

Ineffable flesh, in the pure momentum of vagabondism, I
gained your surprises, your heats, your radiant impieties,
your malevolent absolutes, your crushing ineptitudes, as go
the waves to the last man.

Experience fixed in the evening undressed over absence.

It was just the endearing scheme of a child, a plunder of in-
nocence.

After the ecstatic terrors, I see the white sheets for what
they are, the shimmering port of some fever, the charming
wounds, the funeral teas of stammering crones, the misery of
the long-offended.

No regrets nor dementia from now on. Death sanctified in
their way. It was not mine.

Surely it's not from around here.

TRANSLATOR'S NOTE

Every translation is a kind of forgery. This one also happens to be the translation of a forgery. Although its exact origin remains up for debate today, the widely accepted explanation of this incarnation of *La Chasse Spirituelle* has as its source one of its purported authors: Nicolas Bataille, a stage actor and admirer of Rimbaud whose theatrical adaptation of *A Season in Hell* in 1948 was panned by critics and colleagues.

When I told my friend Selen that I was translating a text born from the revenge plot of a misunderstood thespian against his harsh reviewers, she said "how petty and brilliant", which is perhaps the best way to summarize the cross-purposes surrounding the 1949 publication of *La Chasse Spirituelle*.

Nicolas Bataille's production itself was quite simple. None of the text of *A Season in Hell* was altered, merely rearranged into four monologues spoken by different actors, all meant to symbolize a distinct aspect of Rimbaud's personality. As this resulted in too short a runtime, after each performance the troupe would host small conferences discussing Rimbaud's life and work. They had also sourced relevant books and photographs from the publishing house Mercure de France and set up a bookstand for the audience to peruse, managed by disgruntled librarian Maurice Billot, who would jeer at the stage during the debates, proclaiming that it was nonsense to adapt poetry for the theater. Billot was close friends with Maurice Saillet, who worked with Mercure de France. Maurice Saillet who, despite never having seen the play himself, once told Nicolas Bataille that if he ever discovered an unpublished Rimbaud manuscript, he would keep it a secret so that Bataille couldn't assassinate it like he had done *A Season in Hell*. The consensus among its maligners was that the whole thing was an insult to Rimbaud's name by an amateur. Of course, this reception was most insulting to Bataille, who had intended the production as a love letter to an idol, and in any case thought he knew Rimbaud just as well as, if not better than, his naysayers.

To prove this point, he and Akakia-Viala, a librarian at the Cinematographic Institute who had assisted with set design and costumes for the stage production, concocted a plan to author a forgery - a prose poem in five chapters. They had come across a passage in a book called *Rimbaud Le Voyant* (Rimbaud the Oracle) by Rolland de Renéville indicating the existence of a vanished Rimbaud manuscript - a speculation that Rimbaud's most mystical philosophies must have been expressed in a text called *La Chasse Spirituelle*, which was assumed to have been destroyed by Paul Verlaine's wife in a jealous rage.

In a fortuitous supplement to their ruse, Pascal Pia, writer, independent publisher, and pataphysicist, had recently found out about the existence of an unpublished Rimbaud manuscript in the catalog of erotic bookseller Charles Carrington – the listed item was untitled, but just so happened to be a work of prose in five chapters. The purchaser of the book was never revealed.

Bataille knew that the best way to get the word out about something was to disguise it as a secret. He approached Maurice Billot one night with a compelling tale. Just the other evening, when Billot happened to be away from the bookstand, a respectable old man had come up to tell them how much he adored the play, how it had given new life to Rimbaud's text and he had never seen anything like it in his life. He invited Bataille and Akakia-Viala to get a drink back at his place - he had something to show them. And there, under a glass casing, was the original manuscript of *La Chasse Spi-*

rituelle. Bataille and Akakia-Viala were, according to their manufactured legend, so awestruck that they asked the mysterious stranger if they could copy the text by hand, of course with an accompanying promise of utmost secrecy. And it was with the same promise of utmost secrecy that Bataille was now sharing that facsimile with Billot. No further push was needed. The utmost secrecy extended quickly from Maurice Billot to Maurice Saillet to Pascal Pia to Paul Hartmann, the head of Mercure de France – and they decided, secretly, to publish it.

Bataille was not informed at any point of this chain reaction. He was, in fact, so out of the loop that when he walked out of his apartment one morning and read on the front page of the literary magazine *Combat* that the lost manuscript of *La Chasse Spirituelle* had been discovered and was to be published imminently, he thought to himself how amazing it was that they had finally found the real manuscript. It was only when he flipped through the pages to read an excerpt that he realized the text wasn't the real thing at all, but the forgery he had co-authored with Akakia-Viala. Embarrassed and shocked that what he imagined as an innocent literary prank, something they might end up laughing about over drinks at the Café de Flore, had ended up on the front page of *Combat*, he called Mercure de France, publishers of the forthcoming text, to clear up the misunderstanding.

It is said that it's much easier to fool people than it is to convince them they have been fooled. Whatever reaction Bataille had braced himself for as a result of his confession, it can't have been the scoffing disbelief he was met with. He had intended to destabilize his critics' arrogance, but he assumed that the jig would be up immediately, and at the most he might earn a reluctant admission from his detractors that he knew his Rimbaud after all. Now his friends at Mercure de France were asking him for proof that he was the author of the so-called forgery.

André Breton was the first to identify the text as a fake. He wrote to *Combat* the very day the excerpt was published to say that whoever the author of the purported *Chasse* was, it couldn't possibly be Rimbaud, citing, among other things, a linguistic ineptitude and mediocrity of expression. Breton initially pointed the finger at Pascal Pia, who had authored a Rimbaud pastiche not long ago. As a result, Pia and everyone involved with the publication dug their heels in even further, sparring letters were exchanged in various magazines, and *La Chasse Spirituelle* became the nexus of critical revenge tactics for animosities that had been brewing long before the stage production of *A Season In Hell*, including some sharp words flung between Saillet and Breton in the literary press.

Ultimately, the closest Bataille got to proving that himself and Akakia-Viala were the forgers of the text was much later, during a televised roundtable conference hosted by La Une to discuss this whole affair. Rolland de Renéville, the author of the text in which Bataille and Akakia-Viala had first read about *La Chasse Spirituelle*, challenged them to forge an additional chapter. They in good faith accepted and wrote a sixth poem, *Amours Bâtards* (Bastard Loves). This poem was not included in any subsequent printing of *La Chasse*. Although it was a valiant proof of good sportsmanship if nothing else, it was fairly circumstantial - to this day no one can say for certain that the authors of *La Chasse Spirituelle* and *Amours Bâtards* were identical.

For my part, I have some circumstantial evidence of my own. Although I knew Rimbaud was likely not the author of the text I was translating, the spirit of forgery was infectious, and I started out this endeavor wanting to make the text sound as Rimbaldian as possible – I had a grandiose vision of out-forging the forgery. Inspired by a papercut bloodstain on the Fe-dEx envelope I was using to carry around print-outs of *La Chasse Spirituelle*, *A Season in Hell*, and my working drafts, I had the idea to conduct a little séance and really maximize my psychic proximity to Arthur Rimbaud. When I called upon his spirit he showed up pretty immediately and quite annoyed: "Why should I help you imitate me?" An excellent point, which I somehow neglected to consider before reaching across realms. I was sorry for calling him all the way over for nothing, but could feel him lingering around for a bit anyway, haughty yet curious over my shoulder. Though I can make no claim as to Rimbaud's presence at the time this version of *La Chasse* was first penned, I can say that he was - somewhat begrudgingly - present for its translation.

Emine Ersoy, 2024

LA CHASSE SPIRITUELLE

INTRODUCTION

Parmi les textes inédits et la correspondance que Verlaine, au moment d'abandonner sa femme et son fils, oubliait chez ses beaux-parents, Rue Nicolet, le 7 juillet 1872, se trouvait un manuscrit de Rimbaud intitulé la Chasse spirituelle. *Quelques semaines plus tard, en novembre, Verlaine adressait de Londres deux lettres: la première à son ami Edmon Lepelletier pour l'inciter à récupérer, si possible, les papiers restés à Paris, la seconde à Philippe Burty pour lui réclamer les mêmes papiers.*

Après avoir écrit à Lepelletier, Verlaine avait en effet ouï dire que sa femme avait confié à Burty, pour que Madame Verlaine mère ne fût pas exposée à en prendre connaissance, des papiers jugés

*accablants pour lui. À ces papiers - les lettres << martyriques >>
de Rimbaud - pouvaient être joints les feuillets de* la Chasse spi-
rituelle, *et c'est évidemment dans le dessein de créer une confu-
sion entre ce manuscrit et les lettres de son compagnon de fugue
que Verlaine, contre tout vraisemblance, explique à Burty qu'il
ne s'agit pas là de véritables lettres, mais de pages éparses du
manuscrit de Rimbaud.*

*Faute de connaître la réponse de Burty, on ne saurait dire encore
si, oui ou non, celui-ci détenait ou avait provisoirement détenu
tout ou partie des papiers imprudemment laissés à Paris par Ver-
laine. En revanche, il est acquis qu'il n'eût pas à lui en restituer.
La remise de ces papiers à Burty, si remise il y a eu, ne pouvait
constituer qu'un dépôt conditionnel. Résolue à faire donner à
la rupture de son ménage la sanction d'un jugement, Mathilde
Mauté aurait-elle pu se dessaisir sans restriction d'une corre-
spondance propre à nourrir l'articulat qu'elle produisait dès le 2
octobre pour justifier sa demande en séparation de corps?*

*Il est toutefois permis de supposer que si l'avoué de Mathilde
Mauté tint à utiliser au profit de sa cliente les lettres de Rimbaud
à son ami, il ne dut pas estimer nécessaire de grossir son dossier
du manuscrit de* la Chasse spirituelle, *qui ne mettait point Ver-
laine en cause.*

*Que devint ce manuscrit? Jusqu'ici les commentateurs de Rim-
baud ont semblé le tenir pour définitivement perdu. Depuis
soixante-dix-sept ans, sa présence n'avait été mentionnée dans
aucune collection privée ou publique, dans aucune vente, sur au-
cun catalogue de libraire ou de marchand d'autographes, et les*

plus obstinés chercheurs paraissaient enclins à en admettre la destruction.

Ils avaient tort. Il existe encore un manuscrit de la Chasse spirituelle, *et peut-être même en existe-t-il deux. Pour des motifs qu'il ne nous appartient pas de rechercher, les détenteurs de ces feuillets d'une valeur et d'un intérêt exceptionnels ne se sont pas fait connaître. Puisse la publication qu'une série de hasards nous permet de faire aujourd'hui, les inciter à se montrer désormais moins jaloux du secret de leur richesse rimbaldienne.*

Selon toute apparence, la composition de la Chasse spirituelle *eut lieu au cours du premier semestre de l'année 72. Peut-être l'examen du manuscrit et sa comparaison avec d'autres autographes de Rimbaud permettraient-ils de proposer une date plus précise, mais en l'état actuel des choses force nous est de recourir, pour dater ce texte, à l'interrogation de son style, à l'audition attentive du son qu'il rend.*

La lettre de Rimbaud à Delahaye datée de << Parmerde, Juinphe 72 >> nous incline à penser que c'est en mai 72, et rue Monsieur-le-Prince, que la Chasse spirituelle *fut écrite. Les conseils donnés à Delahaye:*

Ne pas te confiner dans les bureaux et maisons de famille,

Les aphorismes dont Rimbaud les assortit:

Les abrutissements doivent s'exécuter loin de ces lieux-là. Je suis loin de vendre du baume, mais je crois que les habitudes n'offrent pas des consolations, aux pitoyables jours

Relévent de la même éthique que les principes exprimés dès l'ouverture de la Chasse.

Mais là n'est pas la seule analogie que révèlent la Chasse *et la lettre de Juinphe. En dépit du fait que tout fragment de Rimbaud implique, de la part de son auteur, plus de surveillance et surtout plus de préméditation que sa correspondance, on peut reconnaître dans ce récit à Delahaye un son bien proche de celui que font entendre certaines parties de* la Chasse*:*

Le mois passé, ma chambre, rue Monsieur-le-Prince, donnait sur un jardin du lycée Saint-Louis. Il y avait des abris énormes sous ma fenêtre étroite. À trois heures du matin, la bougie pâlit: tous les oiseaux crient à la fois dans les arbres: c'est fini. Plus de travail. Il me fallait regarder les arbres, le ciel, saisis par cette heure indicible, première du matin. Je voyais les dortoirs du lycée, absolument sourds. Et déjà le bruit saccadé, sonore, délicieux des tombereaux sur les boulevards. – Je fumais ma pipe-marteau, en crachant sur les tuiles, car c'était une mansarde, ma chambre. À cinq heures, je descendais à l'achat de quelque pain; c'est l'heure. Les ouvriers sont en marche partout. C'est l'heure de se soûler chez les marchands de vin, pour moi...

Reste à voir quelle place revient à la Chasse spirituelle *non dans l'œuvre - le mot ne convient pas - mais dans l'orage rimbaldien. A cet égard, aucun doute ne peut subsister:* la Chasse *commande et préfigure tout ce qui, dans* Une saison en enfer, *n'affecte pas* *la << Vierge folle >>. Ce n'est pas par une rencontre fortuite que l'épithète de païen à laquelle Rimbaud avait songé pour le livre qui devait devenir* Une Saison en enfer *se retrouve en tête d'une des parties de* la Chasse.

Les références que l'on peut établir d'un texte à l'autre sont nombreuses. Thèmes et images se donnent la réplique:

Je ne crois pas à la famille, au devoir, aux bonheurs garantis par l'estime. *(la Chasse spirituelle.)*

Quant au bonheur établi, domestique ou non... non, je ne peux pas. *(Une saison en enfer.)*

Nos flottes navigueront encore vers les îles lointaines... De qui rêverons-nous? Les casernes déversent leurs flots de héros gourmeux dans les campagnes hygiéniques, mortes d'ennui. Les femmes guettent les invalides avec gratitude. *(la Chasse spirituelle.)*

Ma journée est faite; je quitte l'Europe. L'air marin brûlera mes poumons; les climats perdus me tanneront...Je reviendrai, avec des membres de fer...J'aurai de l'or: je serai oisif et brutal. Les femmes soignent ces féroces infirmes retour des pays chauds. *(Une saison en enfer.)*

Des chansons niaises groupaient des rondes dans ma tête. *(la Chasse spirituelle.)*

J'aimais les peintures idiotes...la littérature démodée...refrains niais, rythmes naïfs. *(Une saison en enfer)*

On pourrait multiplier ces citations, voire les affirmations symétriquement divergentes:

Je suis bien d'ici. *(la Chasse spirituelle,* Infirmités.*)*

Je ne suis plus au monde. *(Une saison en enfer,* Nuit de l'enfer.*)*

De même qu'Une saison en enfer expose la joie la plus fraîche au << bond sourd de la bête féroce >>, la Chasse spirituelle blesse, menace, et blesse indéfiniment le chasseur. La phrase sur quoi elle prend fin (<< Certes il est d'autres rives >>) ne manquera pas de susciter de nouvelles exégèses. Pour notre part, nous nous abstiendrons et d'en fournir et d'en accepter aucune. Nous n'avons jamais cessé de nous enfoncer dans la conviction que Rimbaud décourage systématiquement toute tentative d'interprétation et de mobilisation. Son plus fier propos: << c'est oracle, ce que je dis >>, nargue le lecteur, car l'oracle est ambigu, et Rimbaud en épaissit encore le mystère par une succession de démentis et de refus.

Nul n'a plus largement que lui usé des deux libertés que Baudelaire regrettait de ne pas voir inscrites dans la Déclaration des Droits de l'Homme: le droit de se contredire et le droit de s'en aller.

- Pascal PIA.

VAUDEVILLE

J'ai pleuré jadis sur de vains attachements. Je ne crois pas à la famille, au devoir, aux bonheurs garantis par l'estime. Soupe rance, sucreries fades et angélique parfum des benoîtes armoires. Rejetons les humeurs, les jouets dépareillés - mièvreries acceptées - et n'oublions pas ces précoces malédictions. Ni attitudes complaisantes, ni offices, ni gloire prudente. Plus d'héroïsme ni d'honneur rétribués. Cachez vos sagesses et vos sciences, vos trésors - vos plaies détestables.

J'ai trop remâché vos dédains, vos prétextes, votre patience sans objet. Pourtant, j'ai apprécié les délices aimables - il n'y a pas si longtemps, j'aurais pu aussi fréquenter les grands, plein de rigueur et de principes. Je ne peux plus rire de ces somptueuses vieilleries.

Je m'écarte du souvenir de ces communions d'enfant, de ces féeries ingénieuses. Vacances. Le presbytère de campagne sentait la lessive et j'honorais l'homme cachant les complots de son indifférence sous les fresques merveilleuses. Chère maladie! Je remonte les boulevards gorgés de peuple vacant. Plaisirs vains et mous. L'odeur de nos anges urbains fait pâmer les crémiers de banlieue.

Nos flottes navigueront encore vers les îles lointaines, nouveaux champs d'honneur pour demain. Les empereurs catarrheux cracheront sur les foules endormies. Les pirates, les égorgeurs seront immortalisés. De qui rêverons-nous? Les casernes déversent leurs flots de héros gourmeux dans les campagnes hygiéniques, mortes d'ennui. Les femmes guettent les invalides avec gratitude.

Magie des couleurs écoeurantes, trompettes qui cuivrent de bleus abcès les paumes et les bouches au midi des tueries malpropres et ordonnées. Des générations de communiantes blêmiront encore leur candeur. Nature hideusement docile, ville riche et confortable, arts accessibles, pianos misérables et faux.

Forcenés des heures. Épileptiques, vous vivrez les dangers populaires, bras épais de sang, jambes écartées, lubriques, bouche au sol: dans les soirs de liberté trop humaine.

Sur l'exercice des gestes quotidiens, des transports d'armes et de drapeaux, vers l'écroulement des apothéoses de gloire, vous serez peut-être fatigués dès l'aube funeste des patries authentiques comme les mères.

VACANCES PAÏENNE

Ce jour, renié, égaré, mort à l'espoir des destinées positions, avantages, pourritures d'abîme entrevues - c'était hier sans doute - j'ai fixé l'objet de ces décisions issues de la mystification des débauches.

J'oublierai la saveur de l'anathème, l'insulte simple - pour une fois - toutes les férocités, les frénésies grotesques, les gestes cruels, les vains blasphèmes aussi de l'enfance. Je vois avec ces yeux les déserts craquelés comme les croûtes, écrasés de ciel. Une forêt de soie et d'ambre, mais plus loin. J'entends, pourquoi encore cette trahison du silence où j'entre princièrement, des mélodies inavouables. Faut-il souffrir encore et me traîner jusque là? Je ne pourrai plus boire, mais quelles récompenses exquises hors des limites de ces chairs appauvries. Je fuirai le jour malappris, les pièges familiaux, la lampe des veillées contraintes et menteuses, les digestions acceptées, les bruits paisibles derrière la porte close, la ville exténuée.

Je veux balbutier l'abandon de nos systèmes définitifs, de nos cultures, richesses de nos mémoires. Apprendre désormais l'oubli des fictions consenties, je parle des heures faciles et mortelles, de l'amitié, des reconnaissances pratiques.

Je vénère les animaux indifférents, splendides et errants comme les anciens dieux, sous les cieux impitoyables.

S'abolir, se perdre, sentir sa peau se dessécher sous le regard avide et envieux des curiosités puériles et - sans pudeur - s'engloutir dans les rêves les plus profonds. Le temps: démence des autres! Je ne crierai plus vers vous, repus de sagesse logicienne. Vous ignorerez ces révélations interdites, les rythmes de cet orchestre barbare, ma patience, mon obstination, mon âpre royauté, ma force.

Les déluges engloutissent les peuples supérieurs et seul un couple d'idiots maniaques et bien-pensants peut voir sur les pavois d'une richesse cramoisie les messagers tout fumant de ses devoirs.

Les vieilles grèves s'estompent dans le vent: les prairies fraternelles bruissantes des joies d'insectes.

Je vois sans hésitation des falaises de quartz, gardiennes des vallées noires et rousses, sans fleuve. Je meurtrirai le rêve ordinaire par ruse, science, amours bâtardes et humiliantes douceurs. Et ce sont encore des danseuses, des artistes ridicules et beaux. Donner tout pour un meurtre au petit jour au fond d'un parc à Babylone.

Je tordrai les barreaux d'un ciel occidental et suivrai les traces des mages et des prophètes bafoués, dans l'angoisse de nos parentés englouties. Mais sans filiation aux croyances désuètes, au destin des vertus absurdes et abîmées - libre.

L'épouvante des assouvissements me précède. Je me déferai des gestes élémentaires. Croiser les bras sur l'infini. Comme c'est simple! Les barbares supérieurs avaient tout prévu: liquider la sagesse et en avant!

Bientôt plus d'absence. Les coeurs ne seront plus torturés. Plus de soins. Une force nourrie de silence, immobile. Plus de volonté ancienne, plus d'élans attardés. La plaine implacable. Le corps fixe et vacant comme un sanctuaire. Tourner les yeux sur l'ombre intérieure. Dormir sur le tapis magique et, la tête pleine de terrifiantes réalités - plus léger qu'un rêve d'enfant sage - illusions mystérieuses, je m'effacerai délicieusement.

Nef rehaussée d'or, sans flots, sans tempête, j'aborderai bientôt au port vénéré d'où le soleil s'aventure sur nos continents commerciaux, nos docks, nos marées fructueuses, nos escales, nos mornes plages.

Je veux marcher sur les cordes raides, vers cette sagesse première et ce monde merveilleux.

Mais le coeur révulsé, la tête pleine d'eau boueuse, chasseur lamentable: hantant les berges maladives où s'infusent les dorades. Il me faut encore vouloir par delà les mythes séculaires.

Mes regrets, ma présence divergente, ma froide raison, hélas! Et tous les enthousiasmes et les calculs, et les détours affectueux, économie respectable, plus rien ne me sera compté. Je sortirai, banni pour de bon, ivre, du cercle des actions aux lueurs des arabesques d'épouillées. Je me rappellerai l'odeur aigre des femmes pieuses. Je rêverai cheval. J'adorerai le bouc sacré, les chats griffus miaulant de convoitise.

Je me retiendrai au bec de gaz des quartiers sans espoir, je marcherai jusqu'à l'éblouissement, les pieds en feu, je franchirai les salles successives d'un temple vide incroyablement grouillant et je mourrai en détruisant des tubercules d'or et des oiseaux blancs.

Adieu, catéchisme, amours vétustes!

J'ai tranché ma main droite.

ÉDENS

Dernière prière aux archanges qui pourrissent dans mes forêts fiévreuses. Je titube les soixante vies du cycle. Enfin je fixerai mes affûts, mes poursuites, mes chevauchées - images ordinaires forgées dans le malaise du réveil. Je vous confie mes absences factices, un recueil des mots sauvages qui flambent. J'ai balbutié fameusement à travers les sortilèges pittoresques des sens.

Enfant sordide et compliqué, vautré au pré stupide j'ai secoué les pistils, humé des vapeurs vertes et froides, plongé mes bras énervés dans la vase d'une atroce tiédeur, aux vers roses et gras. J'ai appris les sifflements des monstres, les couples héroïques, les rires de boue des lacs de ténèbres, les floraisons des châteaux d'angoisse où dorment des princes chastes et doux. J'ai compté les pierres précieuses et les rivières aériennes, dressés des statues de sable mouvant aux criques des mers tropicales, hanté les baraques foraines où s'égorgent les ballerines.

J'ai expérimenté les fringales des enfants pauvres. La tête sonore comme un coquillage géant, abandonné aux lendemains de ces orgies de jeûne, l'esprit plus lourd qu'une cathédrale. J'ai interrogé la sagesse des marbres anciens, déchiré les grenades aux formes obscènes et des ruisseaux de rubis coururent sur mes lèvres.

Un corps fumant, âcre. Désir, désespoir, affliction tardive, baisers poisseux de venins exotiques, lèpre, étreintes désespérées. Calice brûlant, airs d'opéra, gladiateurs enrubannés pour les faims populaires, sirènes et sorcières, mariées hypocrites, prêtres buvant des liqueurs douteuses au son d'un tam-tam, sièges rustiques pour les salons. Des bulles glaireuses crèvent devant mes yeux, des flèches multicolores me clouent sur un calvaire de confection. Les sœurs aînées aux agaçantes sollicitudes consolent les enfants pathétiques et les doux Jésus raccommodent les bonheurs usagés.

Paradis comme il faut, Cythère, une main pour me secourir, puis, seul, calme, dans les champs de sainfoin, j'entendrai les cris d'autrefois derrière les arbres, le vent guérisseur des espérances. J'arriverai au sublime degré d'une perfection éhontée. Ne plus cacher au monde mes bévues et mes égoïsmes et ces tendresses inconnues.

Je règle les besognes les plus infâmes.

Cascades de fiel, tourbillon de neige rouge et noire, souffle d'haleines fétides, carnaval, tortues énigmatiques, cancers et hydres fardés de vert-de-gris, chiens géants, coqs châtrés, dentelles; dans le ciel glorieux, des lambeaux de chairs organisent des ascensions, des singes grotesques volent mes vêtements, flèches, ruisseaux de gemmes, fleurs sans formes, sève sanglante, cristaux éclatés, pastels poussiéreux des obscures visions. Les kangourous sautent sur les places publiques et les cargos tressent des chapelets de cordes glissant sur des océans de braise.

Papillons marins, Jamaïques, citronniers, poivriers des tropiques engourdis, algues aromatiques, pustules, plaies de miel, mammouths furieux, serpents en rut dévorant des équipages, fleurs cannibales aux harpons de velours, délices, tortures...Ah!! pitié!

Grâce, je ne recommencerai plus.

Tout cela n'est pas sérieux vraiment.

INFIRMITÉS

Je ne plaisanterai plus avec les fièvres et les cauchemars qui firent trembler mon corps et agacèrent mes nerfs. Je sais ce que je leur dois.

Il fallait rejeter les besoins, les craintes, les doutes. J'aurais splendidement volé la nature et ma race et mes obscurs parents. Je ne suis qu'espèce - rien de plus - lié à ces viscères domestiqués et à cette âme déclassée et funeste. Je suis bien d'ici.

La vie est simple et fructueuse, hors la pensée et cette soif. Saurais-je m'y prendre? Les savants, les laboureurs me cernent au champ de l'action vertigineuse et amère. Les feuilles poussent, les nourritures habituelles se renouvellent et l'eau et le feu. J'ai perdu les traces ordinaires. Je n'aurais pas dû.

Aucune bête ne pourra me soumettre désormais.

Je reviens soumis à l'accueil de la maison austère et confortable. Je fis honte aux mendicités d'amour, à la faim altruiste, aux désirs de présence fraternelle. J'ai entrevu les voluptueuses quiétudes, les yeux cernés de réseaux mauves, orphelin des équinoxes et des marées inévitables, des lunaisons et des lois naturelles. Des chansons niaises groupaient des rondes dans ma tête. Refrains d'école, prières mécaniques utiles à l'hygiène de nos corps adolescents.

Évadé des limites de l'absurde et des ignorances manifestes, dans l'apaisement des mystères étreints, besoins, devoirs, générosités dérisoires, combats stériles seront à jamais perdus pour moi. Que ferez-vous de cet héritage pratique, abandonnés et obstinés idiots, saouls de querelles puériles et séculaires comme vos races?

Les fumées grasses crachent les relents des traversées sans retour, les immondices obstruent l'embouchure des fleuves béants; ventre gonflé, excréments, amer liquide, vestiges gluants des cités monstrueuses.

Les petites filles au regard étonné et bête me font rougir de honte.

Anathème à ces penchants des fertilité diabolique. Nature reine des hordes tu nous as soumis. Des nuits entières j'ai couru après les visions béates - courses de lunes, éclipses monotones, cercles fastidieux - piètre résultat.

Vous qui pratiquez les gestes relatifs et l'effort rémunéré, vous m'oublierez.

Gris cadavres, comment vous sauver pourtant?

MARÉCAGES

Retour au ciel ami de toujours. À la terre d'origine affluent les déceptions fatales après les fureurs ourdies contre les puissances. Banni des capitales prudentes, sourdes aux vérités. Je ravale leurs paroles et leurs poussières, délires de charlatans. Mais les monuments, témoignages de leur incompréhension magistrale, s'écrouleront.

Le temps et ses accoûtrements risibles reprend son cours. Rien ne sera plus que pratique. Les courbes s'évanouissent, les nombres, anciennement domptés, se désagrègent. Hors la prévoyante garantie d'une terre brune et maternelle, chaude comme un oiseau. Peut-être entre la fraternité incertaine, vestige de magies primaires, romance permise. Science, chimie, frénésie, les astres pulvérisés, tomberont en poudre d'or, aux révélations ultimes. Des barques noires dériveront sous quels cieux renouvelés?

Les figues s'écrasent sur les plages de cendre et les nuages infects saccagent les vergers d'éden.

Reprendre outils et lutte au sentie du devoir.

Dimanches cravatés au boulevard de l'ennui.

Dans l'orchestre de jappements cruels, la meute m'a éventré. J'ai guetté l'évanouissement du monde; sans souffle, les yeux tuméfiés de démangeaisons, réglé le rythme des forces dernières. L'éclatement impeccable du feu m'a échappé et tout était intact: royautés comiques, égarements populaires. Cultes, pierres, arbres, coeurs repoussés, vivrai-je encore vos présences insolites - vos fiertés, vos dédains?

J'ai oublié des armes, des ruses, des charmes en cette chasse d'adorable magie. Je reviens aveugle, les mains glacées et mortes, sans proie étincelante à produire, sans trophées, aux clairières funèbres d'arbres déchus. Je me gorgerai dégoûts - et que faire, rendu aux abrutissements magistraux, aux disciplines, aux nécessités de l'époque béante à ces pieds durcis.

Je me suis vu grelottant, accroupi au carrefour des inquiétudes anciennes, en main le sceptre, au front la couronne écarlate, accessoires exigeants des messies. Faut-il se lever aujourd'hui, courir, s'affairer? C'est la vieille mode.

Chairs ineffables, j'ai gagné, dans le pur élan des vagabondages, vos surprises, vos chaleurs, vos impiétés radieuses, vos absolus maléfiques, vos écrasantes inepties, telles les vagues jusqu'au dernier homme.

Expérience figée au soir dérobé sur l'absence.

Après les effrois extatiques, je vis franchement les draps blancs, l'escale rutilante de quelque fièvre, les plaies adorables, les tisanes mortuaires des vielles balbutiantes, la miséricorde des injuriés de jadis.

Ni regrets, ni démence désormais.

La mort sanctifiée à leur manière.

Ce n'était pas la mienne.

Certes il est d'autres rives.

LA CHASSE SPIRITUELLE
BY ARTHUR RIMBAUD

TRANSLATED BY
EMINE ERSOY

PUBLISHED MMXXIV
MERCURIAL EDITIONS
NEW YORK CITY

DISTRIBUTED BY THE MIT PRESS